FALSE FRIENDS

FAUX AMIS

BOOK I

malet@supanet.com
www.elmalet.co.uk

FALSE FRIENDS

FAUX AMIS

Ellie Malet Spradbery

Matador
5 Weir Road
Kibworth Beauchamp
Leicester LE8 0LQ, UK
Tel: (+44) 116 279 2299
Fax: (+44) 116 279 2277
Email: books@troubador.co.uk
Web: www.troubador.co.uk/matador

ISBN 978 1848761 933

British Library Cataloguing in Publication Data.
A catalogue record for this book is available from the British Library.

Typeset in 11pt Palatino by Troubador Publishing Ltd, Leicester, UK

Matador is an imprint of Troubador Publishing Ltd

Printed in Great Britain by the MPG Books Group, Bodmin and King's Lynn

*À Marie-Angèle et à mon cousin Jim Fletcher
pour leur aide et leur encouragement*

*A big thank you to Julie Knott,
my computer guru and IT Consultant*

CONTENTS

Improve Your French and Have Fun!

LIST OF ABBREVIATIONS

adj. : adjective
adj. f : adjective feminine
adj. m : adjective masculine
cf. : compare with (see)
f. : feminine
fam. : familier (familiar, a bit cheeky or rude)
fpl : feminine plural
hist. : historical
hum. : humorous
m. : masculine
lit. : literal
met. : metaphorical
mil. : military
mpl : masculine plural
nf : noun feminine
nfpl : noun feminine plural
nfs(ing.) : noun feminine singular
n.inv. : noun invariable
nm : noun masculine
nmpl : noun masculine plural
pp. : past participle
qch. : quelque chose
qn : quelqu'un
sb. : somebody
sb.'s. : somebody's
sth. : something
svp. : s'il vous plaît

SECTION 1

Beware of False Friends:
'attendre' means 'to wait' and *not* 'to attend'...

FALSE FRIENDS

FRENCH > ENGLISH	ENGLISH > FRENCH
d' *abord* > firstly	*aboard* > à bord
une *accolade* > an embrace	an *accolade* > une marque d'approbation
un *ado* > a teenager	*ado* > l'agitation (nf)
l' *affectation* (nf) > the allocation	*affectation* > la simulation, le manque de naturel
l' *agonie* (nf) > dying	*agony* > le supplice
une *amende* > a fine	an *amendment* > une modification
un *assignat* > a bank note (hist.)	an *assignation* > un rendez-vous
l' *assistance* (nf) > the present company	*assistance* > l'aide
assister à > to attend	*to assist* > aider
assorti(es) (adj.) > matching	*assorted* > différent(es), dans toutes les tailles

un *attaché* >
assistant, officer

attached >
lié(es), joint(es)

attendre >
to expect, to wait

to attend > assister à

les *avatars* (nmpl) >
misadventures

an *avatar* >
une incarnation *and* an
avatar

une *averse* > a
shower (of rain)

adverse >
négatif(s), -ive(s),
défavorable(s)

avisé(es) (adj.) > wise

advised > conseillé(es)

un *bachelier*… > …has
passed the bac.

a *bachelor* >
un célibataire

un *ballon* > a football

a *balloon* > un aérostat

le *banc* > the bench

the *bank* > la banque

les *baskets* (nmpl) >
trainers (sports shoes)

a *basket* >
une corbeille, un
panier

blême >
ashen-faced, livid

to blame >
blâmer, reprocher à

blesser > to
hurt, to wound

to bless > bénir

un *blouson* > a short jacket

a *blouse* > un chemisier
cf. shirt (section 5)

une *borne* > a boundary marker	*borne* (pp of 'bear') > emporté(es)
une *brassée* > an armful	*brasses* > les cuivres (nmpl)
une *brassière* > a (baby's) vest	a *brassière* > un soutien-gorge
une *bribe* > a bit, a snatch (music)	a *bribe, to bribe* > un pot-de-vin, soudoyer qn
la *bride* > bridle	the *bride* > la mariée
le *but* > the aim, the goal	*but* > mais
la *capeline* > a wide-brimmed hat	a *cape* > une pèlerine
capitale(s) (adj. f.) > important	a *capital* (letter) > une majuscule
le *catcheur* > wrestler	a *catcher* > l'attrapeur
la *chair* > flesh	a *chair* > une chaise
la *chaire* > the rostrum, the pulpit	the *chair* > la chaise
le *char* > the tank	a *char* > une femme de ménage

clair(es) (adj.) > light	*clear* > évident(es), lucide(s)
un *cliché* > a photo	a *cliché* > un poncif
un *clip* > a brooch	a *(paper) clip* > un trombone
un *coin* > a corner	a *coin* > une pièce (de monnaie)
un(e) *comédien(ne)* – cf. Comédie-Française > an actor / actress	a *comedian* > un(e) comique
une *commode* > a chest of drawers	a *commode* > une chaise percée
commotionné(es) > (shell-) shocked	a *commotion* > un tapage
compréhensive(s) (adj. f) > understanding	*comprehensive* > détaillé(es), complet, complètes
congestionné(es) > flushed, red-faced	*congested* > surchargé(es), embouteillé(es)
je te *conjure* > I beg you	*to conjure* > faire des tours de passe – passe
la *considération* > admiration, respect	*consideration* > le ménagement

le *corps* > the body

a *corpse* > un cadavre

le *crayon* > the pencil

a *crayon* > un pastel

une *crédence* > a credence table

credence > la croyance, la foi

un *débit* > an outlet (a shop, speech etc)

a *debit* > un point négatif *and* un débit

une *déception* > a disappointment

a *deception* > une tromperie, une duperie cf. déception (section 2)

il a *décliné* (son nom) > he stated (his name)

he *declined* > il a refusé

sa *défense* > his ban, opposition

his *defence* > sa justification

définitivement > conclusively, for ever

definitely > pour sûr, à jamais

un *délit* > a crime

a *delight* > un grand plaisir, une joie

demander > to ask for, request

to demand > exiger, revendiquer

dévider > to unwind, unreel

to divide > séparer (de)

une *devise* > a motto	a *device* > un appareil, un engin
dresser le chien > to train the dog	*to dress* a doll > habiller une poupée
s' *éclipser* > to slip away / to slip out	*to eclipse* > faire pâlir, obscurcir
l' *éducation* > upbringing, manners	an *education* > l'instruction
l' *essence* (nf) > petrol	*essence* > l'extrait
s' *estomper* > to fade	*to stamp* > taper du pied, timbrer (une lettre)
étanche(s) (adj.) > waterproof	*staunch* (adj.) > ardent(es), fidèle(s)
un *étranger* > a foreigner	a *stranger* > un(e) inconnu(e)
faste (adj.) > lucky	*fast* > vite
une *figure* > a face	a *figure* > un chiffre
la *foule* > the crowd	a *fool* > un(e) imbécile cf. foule (section 3)
la *gêne* > uneasiness	a *gene* > un gène

une *grenade* > a pomegranate

a stun *grenade* > une grenade incapacitante

un *grief* > a grievance, a grudge

grief > un chagrin, une peine

gronder > to scold

he *ground* it > il l'a broyé(e)

haïr > to hate

hair > les cheveux (nmpl)

la *hâte* > haste

to hate > haïr

une *histoire* > a story

history > l'histoire (nf)

les *histoires* (nfpl) > trouble, fuss

history > l'histoire (nf)

honnir > to despise

to honour > honorer cf. honni (section 2)

un(e) *illuminé(e)* > a crank

illuminated > éclairé(es)

l' *impasse* (nf) > dead-end, stalemate

impassable > infranchissable

impayable(s) (adj.) > incorrigible, unique

unpaid > sans gages/salaire

l' *impudeur* (nf) > shamelessness/ immodesty

impudence > l'effronterie (nf)

9

un *indice* > a clue — an *index* > une table alphabétique

infime (adj.) > tiny, minute — *infinite* > illimité(es)

une *injure* > an insult — an *injury* > une blessure

inopinément > unexpectedly — *with no opinion* > sans avis, sans opinion

interloqué(es) (adj.) > stunned, taken aback — *interlocked* > enclenché(es) emboîté(es)

un *interrupteur* > a (light) switch — *to interrupt* sb. > couper la parole à qn

un *legs* > a legacy, bequest — *legs* > des jambes (nfpl)

pas *lerch(e)* (old-fashioned) > not much — *to lurch* > tituber / vaciller

une *librairie* > a bookshop — a *library* > une bibliothèque

une *limousine* > woman (or cow!) from the Limousin — a *limousine* > une limousine / une voiture-navette (entre gares etc)

le *littoral* > the coast — *literal* > littéral, au sens propre un *magot* cf. (section 3) > an ape, a nest egg

a *maggot* > un asticot

mince (adj.) > slim, slender

mince > un hachis de viande

la *monnaie* > the change (money)

money > l'argent cf. argent (section 3)

nerveux, -euse > highly strung

nervous > intimidé(es) cf. nerveux (sect. 2)

l' *obédience* (nf) > allegiance

obedience > l'obéissance (nf)

un *pair* > a peer, an equal

a *pair* > une paire

mes *parents* > my relations (parents)

my *parents* > mon père et ma mère

passer outre > to carry on regardless

to pass out > s'évanouir

pathétique(s) (adj.) > sad, yearning

pathetic > pitoyable

un *patron* > a pattern, a boss

a *patron* > un(e) protecteur, -trice

une *perte* > a loss cf. perte (section 2)

pert > coquin(es)

un *polar* > a detective novel

a *polar bear* > un ours blanc

un *pope* > an orthodox priest

the *pope* > le pape

un *portable* > a mobile 'phone

portable > portatif, -ive, mettable

se presser > to hurry

to press > appuyer sur

du *raisin* > grapes

raisins > raisins secs

en *rampant* > crawling

rampant > débridé(es), effréné(es)

la *rate* > the spleen

the *rat* > un rat cf. dilater (section 2)

le *rejeton* > the child (offspring)

to reject > rejeter, repousser

une *réplique* > a line (in play etc)

a *reply* > une réponse

sensible(s) (adj.) > sensitive

sensible > sensé(es), raisonnable(s)

une *serviette-éponge* > a towel

a *sponge (cake)* > un gâteau de Savoie

sinistre (adj.) > forlorn, gloomy, unsettling

sinister > effrayant(es) menaçant(es)

un *smoking* > a dinner jacket

smoking > (en) fumant

le *sort* > (one's) lot, fate

a *sort*/*to sort* > une sorte, un genre/trier

la *suffisance* > (self-)satisfaction

sufficiency > une quantité suffisante

un *surgeon* > a sucker (horticult.)

a *surgeon* > un chirurgien

le *surnom* > the nickname

the *surname* > le nom de famille

un *travesti* > a transvestite

a *travesty* > une parodie, un simulacre

une *veste* > a jacket

a *vest* > un tricot, un maillot de corps

SECTION 2

'Tomber dans les pommes' means 'to
faint'. Don't mention apples…

FRENCH EXPRESSIONS

un	acte de malveillance	a malicious act, vandalism
un	aller-retour/un aller simple	a return (train etc) ticket/a one-way ticket
	anguille (nf) sous roche	something in the wind
d'	arrache-pied	relentlessly
une	assignation en justice	a writ cf. assignat (section 1)
l'	attaché(e) de presse	the press officer cf. attaché (section 1)
	avaler des couleuvres	to swallow an affront, to be taken in, to eat up the miles
	avaler ses mots	to mumble
un	à-valoir	an advance, a credit, to be deducted (from)
un	avion à réaction	a jet (aeroplane)
un	baise-en-ville (care!)	an overnight bag
	baiser la main etc (Note that 'bisou' is 'a peck')	to kiss the hand (take care with 'baiser' as it goes much further than kissing!)

il a	baissé les bras	he gave up, he threw in the towel
	baisser pavillon (nm)	to show the white flag, to give in
	battre d'une encolure	beat by a neck (horse racing)
	battre pavillon (nm)	to fly the flag cf. baisser (this section)
	belle lurette, il y a…	it's donkey's years ago
une	bête de somme	a beast of burden cf. somme (section 3)
	bien entendu	of course
	bille (nf) en tête	straightaway
à	bon escient	advisedly cf. mauvais (this section)
	bon gré mal gré	whether you like it or not, willy-nilly
un	bouc émissaire	a scapegoat cf. tête de Turc (this section)
	bouche bée	open-mouthed, gaping
	bouffer comme un chancre	to make a pig of oneself cf. cancer (section 3)
la	bride sur le cou, avoir…	to be given a free hand or free rein

la	brigade des stups	drug(s) squad
à	brûle-pourpoint	point-blank, without warning
la	carence affective	emotional deprivation
se	casser la figure (*or* la gueule)	to be bankrupted, to go belly up, to come a cropper (to fall)
la	Chambre des communes	the House of Commons
une	chape de plomb	a wall of silence
	chaud comme une caille	as warm as toast, as snug as a bug in a rug
le	chef de pupitre	the head of section cf. pupitre (section 3)
un	chien-assis	a dormer window
	chipoter sur la nourriture	to pick at one's food
	clouer le bec (à qn)	to shut (sb.) up
très	collet monté	very stuffy, strait-laced
les	compliments (nmpl) d'usage	the customary greetings
en	connaissance (nf) de cause	with full knowledge of the facts

de	concert	in unison, together
du	coq à l'âne, passer…	an abrupt change of subject
le	couchant	the sunset, setting sun
un	coup de chien	a squall
un	coup de fil	a telephone call, a ring
un	coup de poing	a punch
les	coups (nmpl) d'encensoir	excessive flattery (!)
son	cuir chevelu	his/her scalp
	débiter des fadaises	to talk twaddle or rubbish
	débordant(es) de confiance	brimming with confidence
une	déception sentimentale	a broken heart, a disappointment in love
	décrocher la timbale	to hit the jackpot
un	délai de rigueur	a final deadline
sans	demander son reste	without asking any questions
sans	désemparer	without stopping cf. désemparé(es) (section 3)
se	dilater la rate cf. rate (section 1)	to split one's sides laughing

	dites-le-moi	tell me (about it)
	donner son aval (nm) à…	to guarantee, to endorse
	de rien	not at all, don't mention it
une	échelle de coupée (gangway, Nautical)	an accommodation ladder
un	élan de tendresse	a burst of affection
l'	enfilade (nf) de maisons	the row of houses
l'	Équipe de France (Les Bleus)	the French football team (!)
	d' est en ouest	east to west
un	état second, être dans…	to be in a trance (to be spaced out)
	états, être dans tous ses…	to be beside oneself with worry or anger
	FAB: franco à bord	FOB: free on board (!)
une	fâcheuse tendance	an annoying habit
en	faction	on duty
il a	failli (tomber)	he nearly (fell)
une	faim de loup *and* la fringale, avoir…	a raging hunger

faire le pied de grue	to hang around waiting
faire les cent pas	to pace up and down
faire un arrêt	to halt (to fasten off a thread)
la faucille et le marteau	the hammer and sickle (reversal)
faute (nf) de mieux	in the absence of anything better
un fauteur de troubles, de désordre	a trouble-maker
un fer à repasser	an iron
du fil à retordre à qn, donner…	to give somebody a headache
(un) fils à papa	a daddy's boy, spoilt
un fin renard	a sly fox
ses fins de mois, avoir du mal à boucler…	to have difficulty making ends meet
fondre en larmes	to burst/dissolve into tears
la force de l'âge	the prime of life
fou de rage	hopping mad (angry)
la foudre et le tonnerre	thunder and lightning (reversal)

ses	frais, il en a été pour…	he was wasting his time, it cost him
au	fur et à mesure	as (one goes along), gradually
à la	gomme cf. à la noix (this same section)	pathetic, crummy, useless
ses	gonds (nmpl), sortir de…	to come off its hinges, to fly off the handle
	gorge-de-pigeon (adj.)	dapple-grey
au	grand dam de qn	to somebody's great displeasure
à	grandes enjambées/grandes foulées	with big strides
	grandeur (nf) nature	life-size(d)
une	grasse matinée	a lie-in, to sleep late into the day
de	guerre lasse	tired of resisting
une	gueule de bois	a hangover cf. langue de bois (this section)
une	gueule de raie	fish face (!)
les	heures (nfpl) de pointe	the rush hour
	hocher la tête/opiner du bonnet	to nod or shake one's head/ to nod (in agreement)

	honni soit qui mal y pense	evil be to him who evil thinks
	hors de lui, d'elle	beside himself/herself (with anger)
l'	hôtel de ville	the town hall
un	hôtel particulier	a (rather grand) private house, a mansion
l'	humour (nm) à froid	deadpan/wry humour cf. humeur (section 3)
	il y a une heure	an hour ago
n'	importe quoi, dire…	to say any old thing, to talk rubbish
un	jardin d'agrément	a pleasure/ornamental garden, even a flower garden (to distinguish it from a vegetable plot)
	jeter l'argent par les fenêtres	to throw money down the drain
du	jour au lendemain	overnight
au	jour le jour	on a day to day basis
	joutes (nfpl) d'esprit	battle of wits
	lâcher la rampe	to kick the bucket
la	langue de bois	formal, stereotyped language, waffle

	lèse-majesté, le crime de…	treason
une	liaison en dents de scie	an on-off relationship
un	lit de fortune	a makeshift bed
un	livre d'occasion	a second-hand book
à la	louche	approximately, roughly
	magne-toi le train (très familier)	shift your arse, hurry up (no trains in sight)
	mal agir	to act badly
le	mal du pays	homesickness
de	mal en pis	from bad to worse
le/la	mal-aimé(e)	an unpopular figure, an unloved person
	manger comme quatre	to eat like a horse
il a	manqué de…	he almost…, he nearly…
une	maquette d'avion	a model aeroplane
la	masse salariale	the payroll
à	mauvais escient	ill-advisedly cf. bon (this same section)
	métro, boulot (*work*), dodo (*sleep*)	the same old routine day after day
	mettre à sac	(ran)sack and pillage

se	mettre en quatre	to put oneself out
	mettre les bouchées doubles	to put on a spurt, work twice as hard
	mille sabords !	blistering barnacles! (hum.)
	mine de rien	casually, with an innocent air
à	mi-temps	part-time
au	mont-de-piété, aller…	to use a (state-owned) pawnshop, pawnbroker's
	nerveux, il me rend…, il m'énerve	he gets on my nerves cf. nerveux (section 1)
à la	noix	pathetic, crummy, rubbish cf. à la gomme (this section)
une	nuit blanche	a sleepless night
d'	occasion, une robe etc	second-hand, a dress etc
d'	ores et déjà	already, from now on

les	papiers (nmpl) gras	litter, rubbish
	pas du tout	not at all, don't mention it
	pas mal/pas mal DE	not bad/a LOT of
	passer outre	to carry on, to neglect, to press on regardless
un	peloton d'exécution	a firing squad
une	pendaison de crémaillère (nf)	a house-warming (party)
à	perte (nf) de vue	as far as the eye can see
un	petit creux (dans l'estomac), avoir…	to be feeling hungry, peckish
en	petite tenue	scantily dressed
une	pièce à conviction	a trial exhibit (exhibit A, exhibit B etc)
	pied à pied	every inch of the way
de	pied en cap	from head to foot/from top to toe (reversals)
à	pied-d'œuvre	ready to get on with the job, raring to go

un	pied-plat (hist.)	a lout, a yob
	pignon sur rue, avoir…	to be well-established
	pile poil	(it fits in) exactly / perfectly
un	pince-sans-rire	someone who uses deadpan humour
	piquer du nez dans son assiette	to nod off (during a meal)
	plein(es) à craquer	full to bursting
un	plein-temps	a full-time job
au	poil !	fantastic! (no stripping off involved)
un	point final	a full stop
au	point mort	in neutral (auto.)
un	portable	a mobile 'phone
	poser un lapin	to let someone down, to stand someone up
	pour y arriver	to get there, to succeed, to manage
	prendre la mouche	to get huffy
	prêter main-forte	to lend a helping hand, to come to sb.'s aid
un	piètre prétexte	a feeble / lame excuse
en	provenance de	from

son	quant-à-soi, rester sur…	to be reserved
un	rabat-joie	a killjoy
	ras le bol, j'en ai…	I'm fed up, I'm sick to death (of it all)
	raser les murs	to keep in the shadows, to hug the walls
à la	régalade, boire…	to drink without lips touching the bottle (!)
	retomber dans l'ornière (nf)	to fall back into one's old ways, to backslide
à la	rigueur	at a pinch, if need be cf. délai (this section)
	rire aux éclats	to roar with laughter, to laugh one's head off
	rond comme une caille	as plump as a partridge
un	rond-de-cuir	a penpusher
	rubis sur l'ongle	cash on the nail
le	sac et la cendre	sackcloth and ashes
une	sacoche (en bandoulière)	a satchel (worn across the body)
	sacrebleu !	hell's teeth! (hum.)

du	sang de navet, il a…	he's spineless
un	sang d'encre, se faire…	to be sick with worry
	sans crier gare	without warning
les	sans-abri (n. inv.)	the homeless
un	saut à la perche	pole vaulting
un	saut à l'élastique	a bungee jump
un	saut-de-lit	a negligée
un	saut-de-mouton	a flyover
	sauter à pieds joints (dans qch.)	to rush headlong (into sth.)
un	saute-ruisseau	an errand/office boy
lui	savoir gré de…	to be grateful to him/her for…
une	scie à chantourner *or* découper	a fretsaw
	séance tenante	at once, forthwith, on the spot
	soupe au lait, être…	to be very quick-tempered

	spécialisé(es) à outrance	over-specialized
	sur ces entrefaites	at that moment, at this juncture
	sur le qui-vive	on the alert
un	sursis à l'exécution	a stay of execution
le	tableau de bord	the dashboard, the instrument panel
	tape-à-l'œil (adj.)	flashy, over-ornate
de	temps à autre	now and then
un	temps de beau temps	a time of good weather
le	temps révolu	past times eg times gone *not* returned
se	tenir à l'écart	to keep out of it
	tenir tête à (qn)	to stand up to (sb.)
la	tête à l'envers	his/her mind in a whirl
une	tête brûlée	a desperado, a hothead

une	tête de Turc	a whipping boy cf. bouc (this section)
un	tic chez lui, c'est…	it's a habit with him
le	Tiers Monde	the Third World
	tiré(es) à quatre épingles	(to be) dressed up to the nines
	tire-au-flanc (n. inv.)	shirker
	tomber à pic	to come just at the right moment
	tomber dans les pommes	to faint
	tomber des nues	to be taken aback, to be flabbergasted
	ton sur ton	in matching shades/tones
	toujours la politesse	why it's always a pleasure to visit France
	tout à coup, tout d'un coup	all at once, all of a sudden
	tout de suite	straightaway
et	tout le bataclan, tout le toutim	the whole kit and caboodle

à	toutes fins utiles	for your information
un	trèfle à quatre feuilles	a four-leafed clover
aux	urgences, aller…	to go to (the) casualty (department)
une	vedette en herbe	a budding actress (star) cf. comédien(ne) (section 1)
une	voiture banalisée	an unmarked (police) car
	veiller au grain	to keep an eye open for trouble cf. grain (section 3)
la	vie ici-bas	life here below
son	vis-à-vis	her/his opposite number
il n'	y est pour rien	it's nothing to do with him
les	yeux battus	to have dark rings under one's eyes

SECTION 3
Thousands of French words are designed to confuse us with multiple meanings...

TWINS, TRIPLETS, QUADS

	abîmer / s'abîmer	to damage, to spoil / to founder, to sink
une	aiguille / une anguille	a needle / an eel cf. anguille (section 2)
une	amande / une amende	an almond, a kernel, a scallop / a fine
une	apostrophe / apostropher	an apostrophe / to harangue sb.
	appréhender / apprendre	1) to fear 2) to grasp / to learn
une	arête / un arrêt	a (fish) bone / a stop, a decision cf. faire un arrêt (section 2)
l'	argent (nm)	1) money 2) silver
une	avanie / une avarie	a snub / damage (to car etc)
	baiser la main / baisser cf. baiser (section 2)	to kiss / to lower
les	berges (nfpl)	1) (river) banks 2) years (old)

en berne/berner	at half-mast/ to fool, to hoax and to toss in a blanket (!)
bondé(es)/ boudé(es)/ bouder	(crammed) full/ shunned/ to sulk
le boute-en-train/ un boutefeu	the life and soul of the party/ a firebrand
un buffet	1) a sideboard 2) a refreshment room
une cachette/une cachotterie	a hiding place/ to keep something a mystery, to be secretive
un cambriolage/un carambolage	a burglary/ a crash, multiple pile-up
la campagne/la compagne	the country(side)/ the (female) companion
un canard	1) a duck 2) a 'rag' (newspaper etc)
un cancer/un cancre/un chancre	cancer/ a dunce/ a canker cf. bouffer (section 2)

une cave/un cave/ cave (adj.)	a (wine) cellar / a plonker (!)/ hollow (adj.)
chanter/faire chanter qn	1) to sing 2) to blackmail sb.
un chapeau/chapeauter	a hat/ to oversee, to supervise
un chapitre/ chapitrer	a chapter, a heading, a subject/ to admonish,to lecture
chiche (adj.) / chiche !	1) mean, meagre, paltry 2) capable/ you're on!
le chiendent/la chienlit	couch grass/ chaos, havoc *and* fancy dress (hist.)
le chœur/le cœur	the choir/the heart
le civet/la civette	stew/1) civet cat 2) chives
un cliché	1) a commonplace statement 2) a photo
un clochard/une cloche	a tramp/a bell
clore, close/ éclore, éclose	to close/to open (a flower etc)

le	colombage/ un colombier	half-timbering/ a dovecote
	commode(s) (adj.)/ une commode	convenient, easy/ a chest of drawers
la	commotion	1) shock 2) upheaval
le	comte/compter	the count, the earl / to count
un	concours	1) a competition 2) aid, help, support
un(e)	congénère/ une congère	a fellow creature/ a snowdrift
	conjurer cf. conjure (section 1)	1) avert 2) beseech 3) cast out 4) ward off
une	consigne	1) an instruction 2) confinement, detention 3) a deposit 4) a left-luggage office
la	couette	1) the duvet 2) bearing (technical) 3) ways (nautical)
	dégingandé(es)/ déglingué(es)	gangling, lanky/ broken, kaput, rickety

un délit/(se) déliter	a crime/ (to disintegrate), to cleave cf. délit (section 1)
dépendre (de)	1) to depend (on) 2) to take down (garlands etc)
une descente de lit/un dessus-de-lit	a (bedside) rug/ a bedspread, coverlet
désemparé(es) cf. désemparer (section 2)	1) helpless, distraught 2) crippled (maritime)
dévêtir/ divertir	to undress/ to amuse, to entertain
un diable	1) a devil 2) a cooking pot 3) a (porter's) truck
discuter	1) to discuss 2) to argue 3) to talk
le double/doublé(es)/ doubler	double, twice as much/ lined (coat etc) / to overtake
le droit/droit de…	the law/the right to…

	ébréché(es)/ éméché(es)	chipped/tipsy, merry
un	élan cf. élan (section 2)	1) an elk, moose 2) a run-up, surge, thrust
l'	ennui (nm)	1) boredom 2) annoyance, problem, trouble, worry
	entendre	1) to hear 2) to intend 3) to understand
une	épaule/épauler	a shoulder/ to back up, support
un	essai	1) an attempt 2) an essay 3) trying out, testing
	essayer/essuyer	to try/to endure, to wipe
le	faste/ faste (adj.)/ les fastes (nmpl)	pomp/ lucky, prosperous/ the annals
une	faveur	1) a favour 2) a ribbon
le	feu/feu mon oncle	the fire/my late uncle
un	fil/un fils (final s tho' singular)	a thread, yarn, wire/a son
la	foire/ foirer/ foireux, -euse	the fair/ to slip, to flunk/ useless, a washout

la	fonte	1) cast iron 2) fount (typo) 3) melting (snow etc)
la	formation	1) forming, formation 2) training, an academic programme 3) (mil.) group
la	foule/la foulée/fouler	the crowd/the stride/ to press, to trample
	galvauder	1) to sully, to tarnish 2) to make hackneyed
le	garçon	1) the boy 2) the waiter
le	garde-à-vous/ la garde à vue	standing to attention/ police custody
	Gênes/Genève	Genoa/Geneva
la	glaise/le glaive	clay/ a two-edged sword cf. sword (section 6)
un	grain	1) a grain 2) a touch of 3) a heavy shower, a squall
une	grenade	a pomegranate/ a (hand) grenade
une	grève	1) a shore, a (river) bank 2) a strike

griffer / griffonner	to scratch / to scribble (down)
grisant(es) / grisonnant(es)	intoxicating / greying (hair)
un guillemet / un guillemot	a quotation mark / a guillemot (bird)
la hâte / un hôte	haste / a guest *and* a host cf. hôte (section 5)
l' heur(nm) / l'heure(nf) / un leurre	good fortune / the hour / a lure, a snare
un hochet / un hoquet	a rattle / a hiccup
l' humeur(nf) / l'humour(nm)	(ill) humour, mood / humour
huppé(es) (adj)	1) crested (bird) 2) swanky (houses, people etc)
interdit(es) (adj.)	1) forbidden 2) disconcerted, stunned
lâcher	1) to loosen 2) to come out with 3) to leave
laisser / lasser (de qch.)	to leave / to tire (of something)
le lierre / la liesse	ivy / joy, jubilation

le lieu/ le lieu jaune	the place/pollock (fish)
une louche/ louche (adj.)/loucher	a ladle, a hand/ shifty/to squint
le loup/la loupe/louper	the wolf/ the magnifying glass/ to miss (a person, a ball etc)
un magot cf. magot (section 1)	1) a Barbary ape 2) cash, loot 3) a nest egg
mal/malin(es)/ mutin(es)	bad/cunning,shrewd/ mischievous
une manche/un manche/ la Manche	a sleeve/a handle/ the (English) Channel
manquer, rater	1) to lack 2) to miss cf. loup (this section)
le maquis	1) the Resistance 2) the bush, the scrub
un marsouin	1) a porpoise 2) marine (mil.)
une massette	1) a bulrush, a reed 2) a sledgehammer
un métier cf. professional (section 6)	1) a job 2) a skill 3) a loom

	mince !/mince (adj.) cf. mince (section 1)	drat (it)!/slim, slender
la	mine	1) expression 2) mine 3) deposit 4) pencil lead
une	montre/montrer	a watch/to show
la	morgue	1) haughtiness, pride 2) the morgue
la	mouche/se moucher	the fly/to blow one's nose
un	mulet/un mulot	a mule/a field mouse
un	navet	1) turnip 2) a third-rate trashy film etc cf. sang de navet (section 2)
	neuf	nine (number)/ new (adj.m)
une	noix/noir(es)	a walnut/ black (adj.)
la	nouvelle/ les nouvelles (nfpl) / une nouvelle	the new girl, woman/ the news/a short story
un	nu/les nues (nfpl) cf. tomber des nues (section 2) / nu(es) (adj.)	nude (art) / the skies / naked
un	numéro	1) a number 2) a character (person)

un objectif/ objectif, -ive (adj.)	1) a (camera) lens 2) a purpose/ unbiased
ou/où	or/where cf. ou… (section 5)
un paraphe	1) a flourish 2) initials 3) a signature
partir/pâtir	to leave/to suffer
pas mal/pas mal DE	not bad/LOTS of
un péché/une pêche/ pêcher	a sin/a peach/to fish
une peinture/une penture	a painting/ a hinge, a strap
pendre/perdre	to hang, to put up/ to lose
une pensée	1) a thought 2) a pansy
une percée/ perçant(es) (adj.)	an opening, a break/ piercing
un percepteur/ un précepteur	a tax collector (boos, huées)/ a private tutor
un périple/une péripétie/ péricliter	a voyage/an event/to be in a state of collapse
une personne/Personne !	a person/Nobody!

un	piquet/piquer/ la piquette	a stake, picket, pole/ to sting, to jab/ cheap, bad wine, plonk!
	pointer	1) to mark off 2) to point 3) to roll 4) to train (on)
un	poncif	1) a cliché 2) a stencil cf. cliché (section 1)
un(e)	porteur, -euse/ un portier	a porter, bearer, carrier/ a doorman
	propre(s) (adj.)	1) clean 2) her/his own cf. own (section 6)
un	pupitre	1) a desk, a lectern 2) a music stand 3) a rostrum
une	pythonisse/ un python	a prophetess/ a python (snake)
la	raie cf. gueule (section 2)	1) a line, a (hair) parting 2) skate, ray (fish)
un	regard	1) eyes, a look 2) a manhole (!)
	regretter	1) to miss 2) to regret
une	remise	1) delivery 2) discount 3) shed 4) postponement
	remiser	1) to put away 2) to bet again

renseigner/se résigner (à)	to give information/ to resign oneself (to)
un requin/un(e) rouquin(e)	a shark/ a red-head
un ringard/ ringard(es)	a poker/ dowdy, old-fashioned
la rogne/rogner	anger/to clip, to trim, to cut down
sabrer	1) to cut down 2) to open champagne (literally with a sword or large kitchen knife) 3) to flunk
le sac cf. mettre à sac (section 2)	1) the bag 2) ransacking
un saint-bernard	1) a Saint Bernard (dog) 2) a good Samaritan (hum.)
un sas	1) (air)lock 2) a double-entrance security door 3) a sieve
une sculpture	1) a sculpture, a wood-carving 2) a tread-pattern (automobile)
un secrétaire	1) a desk 2) a secretary (male)
sentir	1) to feel 2) to smell 3) to taste

un sifflet/ siffler/ sifflets (nmpl)	a whistle/ to whistle/ boos and catcalls
le sol/le soleil	the ground/the sun
une somme/un somme	a sum/a nap, a snooze cf. bête (section 2)
un souci	1) a marigold 2) a worry
souffler	1) to blow 2) to nick 3) to destroy 4) to prompt
la souris/le sourire	the mouse/the smile
le stupre/les stups (nmpl)	debauchery/stupefacients cf. brigade (section 2)
un surin/ seriner	a knife/ to sing the same old song
une syncope	1) a blackout, a fainting fit 2) (music) syncopation
la tache/la tâche/ tâcher	the mark, stain/ the task/ to try
ma tante/tant que	my aunt/as long as
un tapis/tapi(es) (adj.)	a carpet/ crouched, hidden away
un tas/une tasse	a heap, a pile/a cup

le	temps	1) the time 2) the weather 3) the tense (of a verb) cf. héros (section 5)
en	tête	1) in the mind 2) at the head, in the lead
le	tracé	1) a layout, a plan 2) a route 3) a line
la	une/un(e)	front page news/ one (number)
la	veille/vieil(les) (adj.) (also 'vieux')	1) wake(fulness) 2) the day before/ old (NB vieil (adj. m) only used before a noun beginning with 'h' or a vowel. e.g. un vieil homme)
	vingt-quatre/ quatre-vingt	twenty-four/eighty (takes time to unscramble these in mind!)
une	virgule	1) a comma 2) a decimal point
	voir/voire/la voirie	to see/even, indeed, not to say/refuse, rubbish and road maintenance
	voler	1) to fly 2) to steal
un(e)	volontaire/ volontaire(s) (adj.)	a volunteer/ voluntary, intentional, determined

SECTION 4 – Lists

I know that word is a tree…but
which tree…?

TREES

une aubépine	a hawthorn
un aulne or aune	an alder
un bouleau (argenté)	a (silver) birch
un cèdre (du Liban)	a cedar (of Lebanon)
un châtaignier/ un marronnier (d'Inde)	a (sweet) chestnut tree/ a horse chestnut (tree)
un chêne	an oak
un érable	a maple
un frêne	an ash
un genévrier	a juniper tree
un hêtre (pourpre)	a (copper) beech
le houx	holly
un if (cf. château d'If)	a yew (tree)
un mélèze	a larch
un mûrier	a mulberry tree
un néflier	a medlar tree

un noisetier	a hazel (tree)
un orme	an elm
un peuplier	a poplar
un platane	a plane tree
un saule (pleureur)	a weeping willow
un sorbier (des oiseleurs)	a rowan
un sureau	an elder (tree)
un sycomore/ un faux platane	a sycamore
un tilleul	a lime tree/a linden tree
un tremble	an aspen
un troène	privet

BOATS

un bac	a ferry, car-ferry
un bateau à moteur	a motorboat
un bateau à vapeur	a steamer
un bateau/canot de sauvetage	a lifeboat
un cargo/un navire de charge	a freighter
un chaland	a barge, a lighter
un chalutier	a trawler
un contre-torpilleur	a destroyer
un croiseur	a cruiser
une frégate	a frigate
un galion	a galleon
une goélette	a schooner
un paquebot	a liner
une péniche (aménagée)	a lighter, (a houseboat)

une pirogue	a canoe
un radeau	a raft
un remorqueur	a tug
un voilier (un bateau à voiles)	a sailing boat

ANIMALS

un agneau	a lamb
un campagnol	a vole
un cerf/une biche	a stag/ a hind, a doe
un cochon (care! More sexual meaning in French)	a pig
un hérisson	a hedgehog
une jument	a mare
un lapin cf. poser un lapin (section 2)	a rabbit
un loir	a dormouse
une loutre	an otter
un marsouin	a porpoise
un morse	a walrus
un mulet	a mule
un mulot	a field mouse
un orignal/un élan	a moose

un phacochère	a wart hog
un porc-épic	a porcupine
un renard	a fox
un sanglier/un verrat	a boar
une taupe	a mole
un taureau	a bull

FLOWERS

les ajoncs	gorse
une azalée	an azalea
un bleuet	a cornflower
la bruyère	heather
une campanule	a bell flower
une capucine	a nasturtium
le chèvrefeuille	honeysuckle
un coucou (la primevère)	a cowslip (primrose, primula)
une digitale (pourpre)	a foxglove
le genêt	broom
une giroflée	a wallflower
une jacinthe (des bois)	a hyacinth (a bluebell)
une jonquille	a daffodil, a jonquil
un muflier	a snapdragon
le muguet	lily of the valley
un myosotis	a forget-me-not
un nénuphar (un nymphéa)	a (white) water lily cf. Monet's painting ('Les Nymphéas')

une orchidée/un orchis	an orchid/a wild orchid
une ortie	a nettle
une pâquerette	a daisy
un pavot/un coquelicot	a poppy
une pensée	a pansy
un perce-neige	a snowdrop
un pissenlit (Yes. As it sounds!)	a dandelion
une rose trémière	a hollyhock
un souci	a marigold
un tournesol	a sunflower
une vigne vierge	Virginia creeper

FISH

l' aiglefin(m)/l'églefin (m)	haddock
une anguille (cf. anguille - section 2)	an eel
la brème	bream
le cabillaud	cod
le calmar, le calamar/ l'encornet (m)	squid
le carrelet/la plie	plaice
le chien-de-mer/ la roussette	dogfish, rock salmon
le colin/le merlu	hake
un espadon	swordfish
le flétan	halibut
un gardon	roach
un hareng	a herring
le lieu jaune	pollack
le loup (de mer)/ le bar	sea bass
le maquereau	mackerel

un merlan	whiting
le mulet rouge/le mulet	red mullet/(grey) mullet
l' omble (-chevalier) (m)	(arctic) char fish
la perche	perch
une raie cf. gueule (section 2)	skate
la rascasse	scorpion fish
le thon	tuna (fish)
une truite	a trout

FRUIT

un abricot	an apricot
un ananas	a pineapple
une banane	a banana
une canneberge	a cranberry
une cerise	a cherry
un citron	a lemon
un citron vert	a lime
une citrouille/bigger: un potiron	a pumpkin
un coing	a quince
une datte	a date
une fraise	a strawberry
une framboise	a raspberry
une groseille	a redcurrant
une groseille (à maquereau)	a gooseberry
un litchi *or* letchi	a lychee
une mangue	a mango
une mûre	a blackberry

une nèfle	a medlar (fruit)
une pêche	a peach
une pomme cf. pomme de terre (vegetables list)	an apple
une prune	a plum
du raisin	grapes
une reine-claude	a greengage

VEGETABLES

l' ail (m)	garlic
un artichaut	a globe artichoke
les asperges	asparagus
un brocoli	broccoli
un champignon	a mushroom
un chou	a cabbage
les choux (mpl) de Bruxelles	Brussel sprouts
une ciboule	spring onion
la ciboulette/ la civette	chives
un concombre	a cucumber
une courge	a marrow, a squash (and a berk!)
le cresson (de fontaine)	watercress
les épinards (mpl)	spinach
les épis (mpl) de maïs	corn on the cob
un haricot (vert)	a French bean

une laitue	a lettuce
la luzerne	alfafa
un navet cf. navet (section 3)	a turnip
un oignon	an onion
un panais	a parsnip
un petit pois	a pea
un poireau	a leek
un poivron	a pepper
une pomme de terre	a potato
un radis	a radish
un rutabaga	a swede
une tomate	a tomato
un topinambour	a Jerusalem artichoke
une trévise	a radicchio lettuce

BIRDS

un aigle	an eagle
une alouette (des champs)	a lark (a skylark)
une caille cf. rond (section 2) and chaud (section 2)	a quail
une cigogne	a stork
un courlis	a curlew
une crécerelle	a kestrel
le cygne	the swan (cf. Le Cygne - Saint-Saëns)
un faucon	a falcon, a hawk
une fauvette	a warbler
un geai	a jay
une grive	a thrush
un gros-bec	a hawfinch
un hibou	an owl (also: une chouette - several kinds)
une hirondelle	a swallow

un macareux	a puffin
un mainate	a mynah bird
un martinet	a swift
un martin-pêcheur	a kingfisher
un mauvis	a redwing
une mésange (noire)	a (coal)tit
un moineau	a sparrow
une outarde	a bustard
un perroquet	a parrot
un pic(-vert) cf. pivert (below)	a (green) woodpecker
la pie	the magpie (cf. La Pie - Monet)
un pinson	a chaffinch
un pivert	a green woodpecker
un rossignol	a nightingale
un rouge-gorge	a robin (redbreast)
un urubu, une buse	a buzzard
un vanneau	a lapwing/peewit
un vautour	a vulture

SECTION 5

Words that don't fit anywhere else but that I find
interesting…

MISCELLANEOUS

l' addition (nf) /la soustraction, s'il vous plaît	the bill/the bill, humorous version, please
arrêt, bâtard, côte, hôte, pâte, rôtir	ât, ôt, etc often hides an 's': hôpital etc etc
un(e) autochtone	a native, indigenous (adj.)
Balzac	to avoid French titters, pronounce 'Bal' to rhyme with 'Hal' not 'hall'
Bonjour, monsieur/ madame	*always* say this in shops etc
branché(es) (adj.)	plugged in, switched on (lit. and met.)
les bras (nmpl) ballants lit. 'swinging arms'	a difficult one for us: the closest I can get: 'undecided', 'carefree'; also 'empty-handed'
un courriel et l'informatique (nf)	an e-mail and computer science, computing
et... et...	both... and... cf. ou... (this section)
europe1 radio (Paris) 185LW	JUST LISTEN!! And/or visit: www.europe1.fr

	feue Mme Michelak	the late Mrs Michelak cf. feu (section 3)
le	frangin/ la frangine	the 'bro'/ the 'sis'
un	héros, un fils, un rubis, le temps etc	these are *singular* in spite of the final 's'
un	hôte	a host *and* a (distinguished) guest
	lundi, mardi, mercredi, jeudi, vendredi, samedi, dimanche	all these days of the week are masculine
un	malus	a (car insurance) surcharge
tu	me manques	*I* miss *you* cf. manquer (section 3)
un(e)	mélomane	not a nasty disease but a music lover
en	meublant un silence	filling an awkward silence (with empty chatter)
le	mois d'août	you can pronounce final t (to distinguish from ou/où)
	ou... ou...	either... or... cf. et... (this section)
	oh là là !	yes, the French really do say this!
la	particule	the 'de' in a surname eg Charles de Banville

le printemps, l'été (nm), l'automne (nm), l'hiver (nm)	spring, summer, autumn, winter
quand même/ quand même !	all the same, even so/ I ask you! Can you believe it? (Best said with a shrug and a Gallic pout)
a shirt	*une* chemise (man's); *un* chemisier (woman's)
le stupre	debauchery NOT rape as Italian cf. stupre (section 3)
à Sudbury, *dans* le Suffolk, *en* Angleterre	town, county, country
le surmoi	the superego
le temps révolu	time PAST *not* 'come round again'
tous mes amis ; je les aime tous	silent s first 'tous'; sound the s of second 'tous'
tout à fait : completely, entirely	used on its own this phrase can express agreement
ce truc (a useful word!)	this thingie, thingamajig, whatchamacallit?
tutoyer/vouvoyer : (use of 'tu' and 'vous')	a minefield – seek professional help!
végétarien(ne)	do the French find vegetarians weird? (!)

SECTION 6

It can be a good exercise to take an
English expression and translate it
as best one can...

ENGLISH EXPRESSIONS

an	acid smile	un sourire tendu
an	ageing hippie (cruel words)	un hippie sur le retour
	arm in arm	bras dessus, bras dessous
a	bank statement	un relevé de compte
	below average	en dessous de la moyenne
	below sea level	au dessous du niveau de la mer
a	big cheese	une grosse légume
a	bigwig	un gros bonnet
the	black sheep (of the family)	la brebis galeuse (de la famille)
	in cahoots (with)	être de mèche (avec)
	candy-floss	la barbe à papa
a	change of heart	changer son fusil d'épaule
the	cheque was good but the bank bounced	le chèque était bon mais la banque a fait faillite

his	comeuppance, to get…	recevoir ce qu'il mérite
the	corner of one's eye	du coin de l'œil
the	counsel for the plaintiff	l'avocat(e) de la partie civile
a	crank, a dodge-pot	un(e) hurluberlu(e)
a	crazy old coot	un(e) toqué(e), un(e) cinglé(e), dingue etc
my	cup of tea	mes choses favorites
	damage limitation, too late for…	trop tard pour limiter les dégâts
	deafening applause	applaudissements (nmpl) à tout rompre
to	demolish a theory	battre en brèche une théorie
	don't cross your bridges until you come to them	chaque chose en son temps
	down in the mouth	abattu(es)(downcast, demoralized), tout(es) triste(s) (sad, used mainly for children)
	down-and-out	être sur le pavé
	down-at-heel	miteux,-euse(s), éculé(es)
	downmarket	bas de gamme, populaire
	down-to-earth	avoir les pieds sur terre

80

to	eat one's fill	manger à sa faim
an	expert at chess	un maître aux échecs
	famous last words!	on verra bien !
	forewarned is forearmed	un homme averti en vaut deux
	from bad to worse	de mal en pis
	front-page news, to make…	faire la une (des journaux)
it	gets my goat	ça m'énerve
	global warming	l'effet de serre
(to)	Go for it!	Vas-y ! (tenter le coup)
to	go it alone	se débrouiller tout(e) seul(e)
that	goes without saying	ça se voit bien, ça va sans dire
in	good nick	en bon état
the	ground floor	le rez-de-chaussée
	hand-printed	imprimé(es) à la main
a	hat trick (in cards etc)	un brelan (réussir à trois reprises)
	hats off to you, my dear	chapeau, mon cher / ma chère
	Heath Robinson (a contraption)	un truc de fortune

	hold your horses	arrête immédiatement, du calme !
a	hoo-hah	un brouhaha, un tapage, un vacarme
a	hypermarket	une grande surface, un hypermarché
	if it ain't broke don't fix it	ne réparez pas ce qui n'est pas cassé
	I'll never forget whatsisname	jamais je n'oublierai M. Untel
	ill-natured	désagréable(s), méchant(es)
	immediately, or sooner (hum.)	tout de suite, ou plus vite
	into the bargain, to boot	par-dessus le marché, en plus
	just in case	au cas où cf. ou (section 3)
with	knobs on	et encore plus
	knocked me down with a feather, you could have…	les bras m'en sont tombés
a	knotty problem	un problème épineux
a	know-all	M. ou Mlle je-sais-tout
the	language barrier	la barrière de la langue
	look before you leap	il faut réfléchir avant d'agir

he's	losing the plot	il perd le fil cf. fil (section 3)
	made-to-measure	(fait) sur mesure
	made-up	inventé(es), fabriqué(es)
to	make do and mend, to manage	se débrouiller avec ce qu'on a
to	make the grade	se montrer à la hauteur, y arriver
	Mr and Mrs so-and-so/a whatsit	M. et Mme Untel, Machin (chouette)/ un truc
if	need be	le cas échéant
	nineteen to the dozen, he talks	c'est un vrai moulin à paroles
	off the beaten track	hors des sentiers battus
	off-white	blanc cassé
	one thing leads to another	de fil en aiguille
to	overlap, to dovetail	assembler à queue d'aronde, chevaucher
his	own mother!	sa propre mère !
my	parents	les auteurs de mes jours (hum.)
a	pedestrian crossing	un passage clouté
	pigeon-chested	la poitrine bombée
	plain-speaking	le franc-parler or la franchise

	po-faced	à l'air pincé
a	prig(gish person)	un poseur, un faiseur de chichis
a	professional person	un homme/ une femme de métier
to	put one's foot in it	mettre les pieds dans le plat
a	raging ambition	une ambition sans limites
a	reference point	un point de repère
a	restricted area	une zone interdite, une zone à vitesse limitée
a	riddle and a clue	une devinette et un indice
	safe and sound	sain et sauf (reversal)
a	so-and-so	un vieux schnock, quelqu'un de caractère douteux
	soul-destroying	abrutissant(es), déprimant(es)
a	split personality	une double personnalité
the	stairwell	la cage d'escalier
I	stand to be corrected	on peut me corriger
a	stitch in time saves nine	un point à temps en vaut cent
the	sword and the scales	le glaive et la balance

	take it from the top	reprenez au commencement/au début
	tight-lipped	bouche cousue
	unless I'm much mistaken	à moins que je ne me trompe
	until next time	à la prochaine fois
	up to my eyes	jusqu' au cou
a	vital lead	le fil d'Ariane cf. fil (section 3)
	who's calling (on telephone)?	c'est de la part de qui ?
	working one's sock's off	travailler d'arrache-pied, trimer de plus belle

AND FINALLY

Cher lecteur, je te laisse avec du pain sur la planche
(dear reader, I will leave you with this food for thought):

On doit faire attention à ce qu'on veut : ça peut bel et
bien arriver !

Enjoy Your French!